SCOTLAND

THE PLACE OF VISIONS

A SHELL BOOK

SCOTLAND
THE PLACE OF VISIONS

PAUL WAKEFIELD & JAN MORRIS

AURUM PRESS

The photographer and publishers gratefully acknowledge the
assistance given by Shell U.K. Ltd

Photographs copyright © Paul Wakefield 1986
Text copyright © Jan Morris 1986

Published by Aurum Press Limited, 33 Museum Street, London WC1A 1LD
Reprinted 1988
Although sponsoring this book, Shell U.K. Ltd would point out that the author is
expressing her own views.

ISBN 0 948149 19 1

Printed in Singapore

O Caledonia! stern and wild,
Meet nurse for a poetic child!
Land of brown heath and shaggy wood,
Land of the mountain and the flood,
Land of my sires!
SIR WALTER SCOTT

There is no special loveliness in that grey country, with its rainy,
sea-belt archipelago; its fields of dark mountains; its unsightly places,
black with coal; its treeless, sour, unfriendly-looking cornlands; its
quaint, grey, castled city, where the bells clash of a Sunday, and the
wind squalls, and the salt showers fly and beat.
ROBERT LOUIS STEVENSON

Scotland's cauld and grey, you say,
But it's no' ill to prove
Oor dourest hills are only
Rainbows at a'e remove.
HUGH MACDIARMID

LOCH TORRIDON, HIGHLAND

SANDY SLOSS, SANNOX, ISLE OF ARRAN

PREAMBLE

Jagged in the northern sea lies Scotland, and everyone knows about it. Though fewer than five and a half million people inhabit it, though it has no Government of its own, though its native language has mostly been lost and its history is forbiddingly complex, still there can be few literate people in the world who have no Scottish idiom in their minds. The idea of Scotland is very potent, and like some magnificent collage it is made up of a thousand bits and pieces, slabs of truth, streaks of falsehood, fragments of memory and long sad passages of desire.

Until the Middle Ages Scotland was not a nation at all, but a muddle of separate peoples – Picts, Norsemen, Celts, Angles, and perhaps a strain older than them all bequeathed by the neoliths of prehistory. The 30,000 square miles of its mainland (which is shaped something like the bent shoulders of an aged chieftain, or a weary shepherd) were divided among rival kingdoms: the 700 islands were split among many more, and some of them indeed were subject solely to themselves. It took many centuries to make a whole of it, and almost into modern times the history of Scotland was a bewilderment of feuds, conspiracies, kidnapping, murders, battles between earls, wars against England, alliances with France, more wars against England – the whole turbulent drama stalked through by terrible magnates like the Lords of the Isles or the Black Douglases, and illuminated by figures of grand romance like Robert the Bruce or Mary Queen of Scots.

INVERPOLLY FOREST, HIGHLAND

CORRIE, ISLE OF ARRAN

It was in the eleventh century that a king first called himself King of Scotland; in the fourteenth that a governing dynasty was established; but not until the seventeenth century did Scotland as we think of it now come fitfully into being. The Reformation made it a sternly Protestant country. The accession of James VI of Scotland to be simultaneously James I of England irrevocably linked its destinies with London. In 1707 a voluntary Act of Union made England and Scotland one, abolished the Scottish Parliament and put paid to Scottish independence for ever – the 'end o' ane auld sang', as somebody sadly called it. The last reckless fling of Scottish liberty was the rising in 1745 of Prince Charles Edward Stuart, Bonnie Prince Charlie. Today, except for matters of law and education, Scotland is governed from London, and Scottish sovereignty is subsumed in the political identity of Great Britain.

The national status of Scotland, then, is new – not much older than the United States of America – but the world's conception of the country is inextricably mingled with far, far older allusions. We think of Scotland as part of the United Kingdom, with its proud regiments of the British Army, its close links with the British Crown, its eminent representatives at Westminster, and the inescapable contribution it has made to British history; but we think of it also in mistier terms, magic narratives of folk-lore, dim shifting figures of soldiers, queens and sages, the haunting echoes of the Gaelic tongue, the roar of wild seas and the silence of high bleak landscapes.

Then again, the idea of Scotland has been stupendously burnished and distorted by patriotism. When Dr Johnson went to Scotland in the eighteenth century, he expected a country rude and primitive, and rude and primitive by and large he found it: 'Seeing Scotland, Madam,

LOCH NAN UAMH, SOUND OF ARISAIG, HIGHLAND

is only seeing a worse England. It is like seeing the flower gradually fade away to the naked stalk.' Half a century later the patriots, led by the towering propagandist Sir Walter Scott, had transformed this reputation, illuminating everything Scottish with a flame of pageantry. The Highland clan and its symbols, the Lowland chieftain and his feuds, the brave piper, the loyal ghillie, the landscape, the seashore, the ancient language, even the flora and fauna caught imaginations everywhere, brought Mendelssohn to Fingal's Cave, Landseer to the Glen, Queen Victoria to Balmoral, and still move us to this day – is there a man with soul so dead he does not thrill to the skirl of the pipes?

It is all perfectly true, and yet it is not true. Those things exist, are fine to witness, and play their proper part in the consciousness of the nation. But the vast majority of Scots people have nothing to do with clans or chieftains, never wear a kilt in their lives, speak not a word of Gaelic and live in a town. When we close our eyes and imagine Scotland, we are likely to perceive the wild and glorious Highlands, the surf-foamed Hebrides; but much of Scotland is gentle lowland country, and much more is heavily urbanized. In Scotland definitions are often ambivalent, conceptions are often slanted, fact and legend overlap.

I am susceptible to all of it. I live in Wales, so that Scotland stands always in my mind as a bold Celtic comrade to the north – a storm-swept, sea-beaten, epic place, thrillingly to be discerned on clear days from mountains near my home, and speaking of matters immemorially ancient, strange and holy. I love a touch of swagger, too, so that I all too easily respond to the lament of the pipes and the flutter of old flags.

On the other hand I am attracted to an aspect of Scotland that is

GLEN NEVIS, HIGHLAND

CASTLE STALKER, LOCH LINNHE, STRATHCLYDE

seldom portrayed in the tourist literature: the nervous intensity of the Scottish temperament, which finds its epitome in the cities. This is the urgent, sharp, ironic side of the national personality – not at all what Scott commemorated or Mendelssohn loved, but high-flown in another way, for it is at once defiant and compassionate. If Walter Scott, Robert the Bruce, Bonnie Prince Charlie and a thousand other gleaming magnificoes stand on one side of the Scottish divide, they are easily balanced by the iconoclastic genius of Robert Burns upon the other.

So there are Scotlands and Scotlands: Scotlands in the mind, Scotlands on the ground, historical, factual Scotlands and Scotlands devised, embellished or wished-for – all shared out, like booty, between the rival realms of image and reality. Their great common factor is the landscape, and more than most peoples Scots have been moulded by the substance of their country; by the rich glens and rivers of the south, by the famous towns and cities of the centre, by the hard mountains of the north, by the seas and the islands all around. In writing a text for Paul Wakefield's photographs I have accordingly worked geographically, in glimpses and episodes from Border to Hebrides, hoping to find in the nature of the place itself some fusion of the realms; but I have not, by some fortunate alchemy of travel, stumbled upon any all-embracing truth about Scotland. For that you must look beyond image and reality alike, into the third and more recondite realm of essence or suggestion. Between the lines of this text you may perhaps detect something of the ambiguous diversity of the country; but it is between the lines of the pictures that you must search for Scotland's visionary whole.

GLASHVIN, ISLE OF SKYE

ONE

On a fine high September day I crossed the frontier out of England into Scotland, and found nothing at all to tell me so: no notice of welcome, no fluttering flag, not even a bald announcement of arrival or a warning that I had passed from one legal system to another. Perhaps vandals had destroyed the sign. Perhaps souvenir-hunters had removed it. Or perhaps, since along that frontier the transition from one country to another is blurred, Scots people and English sharing a history of immemorial give-and-take, hit-and-run and intermarriage – perhaps in some districts the local authorities thought a sign unseemly. In any case it did not much matter. The border may be a little indeterminate, but just as no country on earth projects a figure more absolute than Scotland's, so there are few which are more instantly recognizable upon the ground.

Almost the first building I saw was one of those gaunt Scottish structures which are half-way between castles and country houses, cluttered about its foot with farm buildings like a chieftain among his serfs. Almost the first animal I saw was a lithe and springy Shetland sheepdog. The first statue depicted a young blood of the country, *circa* 1514, waving a banner he had just captured from the English, and looking rather like a young colonial from the Boer War, or an Australian sheephand in a film. The first family comprised a trim and respectable young housewife in a tartan skirt, a baby in an extremely expensive-looking pram and a husband in leopard-skin trousers and a silver-studded leather jerkin.

MACHAIR AT HOWMORE, SOUTH UIST, OUTER HEBRIDES

CHRISSY MCGILLIVRAY, ISLE OF MULL

JOHN LAING, DUNVEGAN, ISLE OF SKYE

The first shopkeepers I encountered all had that expression of slightly puzzled concern, terrier-like, which I think of as characteristically Scottish. The first small boy I saw looked, as Scottish small boys do, old beyond his years, ageless almost, highly shrewd and rather sceptical. The first conversation I had was with a retired mill-worker sitting at the next table in a coffee shop. White-bearded and eagle-eyed, he was feeding himself upon a plate of fried potatoes and a glass of milk, and told me almost before I sat down that at a house just down the road Robert Burns had once turned up unexpectedly in the middle of the night. He spoke of the incident as though it were yesterday – 'Oh they were very surprised, *verry* surprised to find him there. Robbie Burns himsel', well gone midnight too!'

No, I concluded as I put away my notebook, perhaps a sign at the border would have been superfluous anyway. There was no mistaking where I was. Everything around me, even so close to England, proclaimed this to be Scotland: the look of the place, the feel of it, and perhaps above all the sound of it, exemplified by that old man's cracked but sprightly voice. There are Scots of many dialects, of course; there are Scots who speak Gaelic, and Scots who speak Lallan, the all-but-a-language of the south, and Scots who speak the purest English; but still the generic Scots manner of speaking, which is I suppose the Scots manner of thought, simultaneously welcomes, confuses, baffles and entertains the stranger from the very start, bewitched as it is by strange usages of the country, couched in intonations all its own, and spiked with glottal stops.

The sounds may be exotic, but the scenes of the southern Lowlands seem at first sight reassuring. For centuries, almost into modern times,

BRACKEN ON THE RIVER FINDHORN, HIGHLAND

TWEEDSMUIR HILLS, BORDERS

this countryside was raged over by warring factions, Celts against Norse and Angles, Scots against English, chieftain against chieftain, skirmish and banditry and blood-feud and cattle-raid. Now it seems quite particularly calm and civil. Fine, ample rivers roll as through parkland between the hills. Comfortable farms abound, and enviable country houses. Only ruined castles and shattered abbeys speak of furies long ago, and the little country towns of the south look all homely conciliation, all tables-laid-for-tea.

The territorial compulsion was always strong in these parts, where even an out-and-out criminal like Johnnie 'Black Jock' Armstrong, boldest of the Teviotdale rustlers, lived until they hanged him in a castle of his own. It is down-to-earth country, and its instincts feel earthy too. Rugby football, muddiest of games, is the favourite public pastime, and the chief public festivities are the antique ceremonies of the Rides, in which the citizens of the several southern towns, led by their Cornets, their Standard Bearers, their Whipmen or their Lads, process on horseback around the municipal limits, symbolically establishing their rights of settlement.

If it was exceptionally virulent country in war, it has been notably diligent country in peace, beautifully tended, where splendid sheep are raised and famous clothes and woollens weaved. For a concentrated dose of this organic dedication, try visiting one of the larger farming villages which are distributed all through these southern counties – Moffat, say, a sheep-farming centre which lies in a happily sheltered declivity of the Tweedsmuir Hills. This is an extremely domestic, comradely and rational little place. Its main street is like a French market square, lined with trees, and on both sides of it homely and sensible establishments are ranged. There is a dainty town hall

NEAR THE RIVER ESK, TAYSIDE

JAMES FLETCHER, BREAKISH, ISLE OF SKYE

with pillars, and a tower with an illuminated clock, and a war memorial, and four or five welcoming hotels. At the bottom of the street the Royal Bank of Scotland, clad in probity and dark red sandstone, sternly surveys the scene; at each end of town is a church. There are lots of old-fashioned provision shops, greengrocers, ironmongers, bakers and a café serving home-made scones, and at the Moffat Toffee Shop Mr Blacklock, the third generation of Moffat toffee-makers, offers a selection of 285 kinds of sweets, each in a different jar.

Half-way down High Street, between the post office and the town hall, there stands in effigy upon a high plinth not J. L. McAdam the inventor of tarmac, who is buried in Moffat, not James 'Ossian' Macpherson the poet-forger who devised some of his antique peoms here, not even one of the Earls of Hopetoun whose house is now the Moffat House Hotel, but a more immediately recognizable champion of Lowland values and functions, a big bronze ram.

Perhaps it is because of the mingled historical heritage, rip-roaring adventurism beside domestic providence, that so many of the great Scottish writers have sprung from these southern soils. You can visit the shades of three of the greatest in a single day's pilgrimage – it is never much more than a hundred miles from east to west of the southlands. First, of course, through the crowd of tourist buses always lined up in the car park, to Abbotsford on the Tweed, home of that Scott of Scots, Sir Walter. This is one of the great literary destinations of Europe, one of the principal founts of Scottish reputation, and it also offers a touching insight into Scottish character: for just as Scott personally brought into being a Scotland theatrically heightened and new-coloured, so through the medium of Abbotsford he transformed himself from a man of the bourgeoisie into a full-blown southern laird.

Abbotsford was a modest farmhouse when he bought it, frankly named Clartyhole, or Dirty Place, but he made of it a half-baronial, half-monastic mansion. With its rooms full of antlers and armour, its peacocks in the garden, its coats of arms and its private chapel, it is mostly sham – 'the most incongruous pile', Ruskin called it, 'that gentlemanly modernism ever designed.' At the same time it is endearingly genuine, and for myself, the longer I wander around its preposterous grandeurs, the more I warm to it. The Scotland that Sir Walter imagined has survived for ever after, sometimes more convincingly than the less lofty Scotland of fact: and he himself really did become a great gentleman, as he deserved, there among his escutcheons, his books and his royal mementoes above the river.

Hardly half an hour to the west, and you are driving up a narrow unpaved lane to the home at Brownsbank, near Biggar, of Hugh MacDiarmid, born Christopher Grieve, the most celebrated Scottish poet of the twentieth century and one of its most contentious characters. MacDiarmid's home is the very antithesis of Abbotsford, but is no less movingly embedded in the nature of the country – an old crofter's cottage, set in a rough field beside the lane, with miscellaneous outhouses attached and a glass porch full of potted plants.

MacDiarmid's widow lives there still, and the house is snug, low-ceilinged, bookish, picture-hung, instinct with the quirky fun of the poet, and with memories of the long line of pilgrims who found their way here down the years. MacDiarmid was southern Scottish through and through, so difficult and provocative in some ways, so merry and

GLENTROOL FOREST, DUMFRIES AND GALLOWAY

STEWART LAMBIE, GLEN SHURIG, ISLE OF ARRAN

sweet-natured in others. He even looked the quintessential Lowlander, with his huge striking head, his bird-like postures and his blazing eyes – 'an eaten an' spewed lookin' wee thing,' his own mother thought, 'wi' een like twa burned holes in a blanket.' His personality is all-pervasive, almost tangible at Brownsbank to this day, and on a paving-stone beside the door, as if engraved on the matter of the land itself, is carved the best-loved of his lyrics:

The Rose of all the world is not for me,
I want for my part
Only the little white rose of Scotland,
That smells sharp and sweet – and breaks the heart.

And so, on an even more frequently trodden road, to a house more famous than MacDiarmid's, more reverently approached even than Scott's – the low, thatched cottage at Alloway, on the coast near Ayr, where was born in 1759 the darling of his people, the emblem of his nation, the hero of every retired mill-worker's favourite anecdote, the one writer of whom every living Scotsman knows a line or two, if only 'Auld Lang Syne' or 'A man's a man' – Robert Burns. There is probably not a poet in the world, writing in any language, so beloved by his compatriots as is Robbie Burns of Alloway. In the absence of any triumphant festival of Scottish sovereignty, the birthday of this minor functionary and incompetent farmer, Burns Day, is to Scotland what Independence Day is to the United States or Bastille Day to the French.

There is not much numen to the little whitewashed cottage now – it has too long been sanitized and veneered by tourism – yet never-ending streams of devotees wander star-struck through its rooms or linger on the high-arched Brig-O'Doon nearby, quoting stanzas to each other. It is hard to feel the presence of the poet himself, in a site so thoroughly and repeatedly done over, yet not just in Alloway, but anywhere in southern Scotland his influence and his example can be sensed. Burns's hold over his people is one of the great phenomena of literature, and raises in my own mind fascinating doubts about the popular reputation of the Scots.

For what does it say of such a famously ambitious nation that its paragon of paragons, admired beyond all statesmen, soldiers or sportsmen, should be this homely scribbler? Why does so practical and hard-headed a people respond so easily to his often sentimental views, and sympathize so readily with his financial ineptitudes? What do the elders of kirk and chapel think of his complex sexual life? What do the sycophants or kings and chieftains make of his sturdy egalitarianism? When I was in Alloway once I bought a selection of his poems at the souvenir shop, and read them aloud in my bath in all the glory of their commonsense and kindness –

> *My Son, these maxims make a rule,*
> *An' lump them aye togither;*
> *The Rigid Righteous is a fool,*
> *The Rigid Wise anither . . .*

Or –

> *For a' that, an' a' that,*
> *It's comin' yet for a' that,*
> *That man to man the world o'er*
> *Shall brother be for a' that.*

LICHEN AT THE STORR, ISLE OF SKYE

CULBIN FOREST, NEAR INVERNESS, GRAMPIAN

And I resolved that night, as I lay there soaking, that I would never presume to judge the Scottish character without remembering that somewhere in every Scot, however improbable it seems, a Robbie Burns is hidden.

Great landowners have traditionally dominated the south of Scotland, where the storied clans have no part to play, but where medieval chieftains, having achieved their wealth and status by stealth, courage, luck and braggadocio, passed it down by primogeniture through the centuries of peace. Everywhere in these southern counties long demesne walls, tidy lodges, obelisks on hills and coppices of fine trees show where a laird lives, when he is not away in England. Let us visit one of these patricians, bearing in mind that though his family is in Debrett's now, its fortunes were made by robbery with violence.

We will call him the Colonel, because he is sure to have been a soldier in his day. His family has been here for several hundred years, but he lives unostentatiously, and we are greeted on arrival with a homely plate of scones and raspberry jam, and a pot of tea in a blue flowered teapot beneath a bobbled cosy. The Colonel eats and drinks his ration with enthusiasm, but very soon afterwards fetches a bottle of whisky from the sideboard and pours a couple of glasses – 'Wine of the country – I always say, you should drink the wine of the country.'

He looks like an Irish deerhound, very tall and elongated, his figure only slightly stooped with age, his thin narrow face, clean-shaven, leaning backwards as it were over a tall sloping forehead to his hairline. His eyes are sunk deeply in their sockets, his arms are very long, his hands delicate. He is dressed tweedily, with shoes that look hand-made. At first sight he might not appear to be Scottish at all: but after a while, through that expensively Anglicized exterior, there begins to show something pricklier, more gingery, more ruthless perhaps, and I realize that in fact I am talking to a man almost aboriginally Scots.

We will not even explore his political opinions, so uncongenial would they surely be to a Welsh republican like me, but on every other subject under the sun this descendant of horse thieves is a delight. His memory is prodigious, his stories are comical, his attitudes are mellow. His subjects range from Bonnie Prince Charlie ('all those Stuarts were a rotten lot') to the price of claret ('I used to get it from a man I know in Bordeaux, but now I just go to the supermarket') to snooker on TV ('they're very sporting fellows, extremely sporting'). He quotes comic verse at length and without hesitation. He alludes every now and then to some duke, marquis or other ('by way of being a relative of mine') but only to tell a quaint tale about him, discredit a medieval anecdote or explain the genesis of a family portrait.

It is raining when we leave the Colonel, but he comes to the bottom of his front steps to wave us away; and as we turn the corner of the drive we glance in the driving-mirror to see that old inheritor of blood-feud and cattle-raid regain the shelter of his door, as though he is escaping a royal posse, in a single mighty stride.

His predatory style is proper to the place. This southern country is not all as relaxed as it seems at first. It has been tempered in conflict, and somewhere behind all its manifestations, behind the poetry and the romance, behind the ingrained sense of comradeship, behind the welcoming intimacy of the little towns – behind it all there lies an unyielding, unforgiving streak.

The landscape itself is by no means all gentle valleys and smiling

fields, as the guide-books seem to show, and as it often appears to strangers driving up the easy roads from England. Nature is not always kindly here. The sea-line, never far away, is anything but cosseting. The fishing villages of the east coast are tough, brisk North Sea places, jammed together for shelter above their stony havens; and on the other side, along that south-western hump of Scotland which impends over Solway Firth and the Irish Sea, the coast can be terrifically austere. There is a glowering grandeur to it – low flat empty shores, duny, reedy, quick-sanded, swept by wind and rain from the west, where spindly seabirds poke about in mudflats and old wooden boats lie derelict when the tide goes out.

Inland too, just off any high road, just over any friendly well-ploughed hill, there lies open heathy country, bare, exciting and often mysterious, with solitary upland lakes, spectacular waterfalls and evocative names upon the map – Grey Mare's Tail, Devil's Beef Tub, Mirk Side, Forest of Ae . . . Once I made a winter journey to the birth-place, Leadhills, of the sweet-natured Scottish poet Allan Ramsay –

My Peggy sings sae saftly,
  When on my pipe I play,
By a' the rest it is confest,
By 'a the rest that she sings best . . .

I fondly expected it to be as gentle as his genius, but it was most distinctly not. Leadhills is said to be the highest village in Scotland, and I believed it. Built in clefts and shelters of the harsh hills, its rows of single-roofed houses pitched this way and that, it seemed to be half-pressed into the earth by the winds. Outcrops of grey rock gave a

ON THE RIVER FINDHORN, HIGHLAND

LOWTHER HILLS, EAST OF AYR, STRATHCLYDE

raw menace to the scene, I thought, and the people looked utterly indigenous – men sunk into their greatcoats against the cruel cold, women in flowered pinafores crowding resolutely around the mobile grocer's van as though they were gearing themselves, even on that sunless Monday morning, for inflexible bargaining – not singing sae saftly, it seemed to me, not singing sae saftly at all!

And what could be more bitterly evocative than the castle of Hermitage, if you come to it the right way? To this isolated fortress in Liddesdale, four hundred years ago, impetuously rode Mary Queen of Scots to visit her wounded lover Bothwell, and for the best effect one must approach it as she did, out of Teviotdale in the west: through hills treeless and shadowy, preferably in a suggestive evening light – the narrow road twisting and turning, the hills all silent, cattle on the distant slopes, until there stands before you suddenly the squat and roofless fortress. A stream runs in front of it, lined with trees, but behind its walls a long slope of moorland rises bleak and stormy to the skyline. It is all black romance, all memory and reproach, like a watch-tower of all these southlands.

Driving to Hermitage once myself, on just such an evening, I found a horse-box parked beside an especially lonely stretch of road. When I approached it a man climbed from its cab and opened its wide side doors, and inside, standing sideways to me, I saw an altogether motionless white horse. As I drove past, the ghostly shape of this creature was thrown into silhouette, against the dark interior of the vehicle, by a sudden gleam of the setting sun. In a moment I was gone, but the vision so theatrically revealed then, for so brief a flash, remains to haunt me still. Did I really see it, on the road to Hermitage? Is it waiting there still? Whose horse was it – and when?

CULBIN FOREST, GRAMPIAN

THE LAMMERMUIR HILLS, LOTHIAN

TWO

In a swathe across the neck of Scotland, from the Firth of Clyde in the west to the Firth of Forth in the east, nearly two-thirds of the Scottish people live in towns, cities and suburbs. Here are the coalfields, the shipyards, the steel mills, the factories which made Scotland rich a century ago: here are the industrial complexes, the power stations, the high-rise blocks, the shopping centres, the soccer teams, the lung cancer, the heart disease and the drug addiction, the symphony orchestras and the unemployment of today. Like the Australians, another people we think of as people of the open spaces, the Scots are primarily town-dwellers, and for most of them their glorious rural landscapes serve chiefly as backgrounds, escapes, spiritual props or reminders of their origin.

Almost in the middle of the urban belt, beside the M80 motorway, there stands a massive and convoluted symbol of Scottish urbanism. It looks partly like an aircraft carrier, and partly like an oil refinery, and partly like an uncompleted fortress, and perhaps just a little like the Pompidou Centre in Paris. Outside it is hugely square-built, inside it is all labyrinthine corridors and shopping levels. It is the town centre of Cumbernauld, one of the New Towns built in Scotland since the Second World War, much admired by urban theorists a decade or two ago, and pictured in nearly every book about town planning.

At first you may think it rather a grim symbol, and at closer quarters its peeling paint and unwashed windows are no more encouraging. But I think there is something properly Scottish to it, and its combination of massive external strength and inner complexity really does seem to suit the national temperament. The Scots are adept at urban living, and Scottish life is focused upon towns, just as the widely dispersed terraces and housing estates of Cumbernauld look figuratively towards that central hump. No doubt the severity of the Scottish climate makes towns and cities all the more important; and perhaps too they have provided for ordinary people down the ages some fulcrum of populist loyalty, separate from feudal allegiance.

Whatever the reason, the towns of Scotland are unusually fine. Even the smallest mill town or market centre has an air of consequence, and is likely to be ennobled by an ancient monument, a Victorian hotel, a classical assembly room, or a memorial to some soldier or poet, lawyer or divine, who brought lustre to the burgh in times gone by. Jedburgh (population 2000) has not only an ancient abbey, but an imposing model prison too. Kelso (population 5000) has a magnificent bridge, prototype for London's original Waterloo Bridge. Haddington (population 8000) has a splendid town hall by William Adam and a most harmonious town centre. Stirling has its stately castle and its towering Wallace Monument, Montrose its latticed steeple, Elgin its great cathedral ruin and its suave town houses, Oban its huge uncompleted museum-tower, Inverary its stronghold of the Dukes of Argyll, and many a less eminent place, when you drive into it at the end of a long day, greets you with an air of well-bred worldliness and generosity – urbanely, in fact.

Perhaps among them all the most movingly and even arcanely Scottish is St Andrews, on the lowland coast of Fife. This miniature city (population 11,000) is urbanity itself. Its shape is compact, its situation beside the sea is delightful, and it has everything a Scottish municipality could demand: not just an agreeably functional commercial centre, and an ancient university whose students cycle around, as students should, in scarlet gowns, and an active small fishing port, and a castle, and a ruined cathedral, and a holy legend (the bones of St Andrew are supposed to have been brought here in AD 347) – not just all that, but a civic asset of almost transcendental Scottish value as the world headquarters of the game of golf.

In Scottish terms this is comparable to Rome's possession of the Vatican, Agra's of the Taj Mahal. It means that a whole national ethos finds its symbolic summation in the place: for with whisky, the poems of Burns and the novels of Walter Scott, golf is Scotland's most universally celebrated product. The Old Course, the original of all golf courses, sprawls by the sea at the northern edge of the city, recognizably still the stretch of sandy grassland on which, five hundred years ago, the burghers first entertained themselves with ball and stick. It is an enchanted territory, and all around it spell-bound dependencies are assembled: three other golf courses, at least five other golf clubs, a clutch of golfing shops, golfing outfitters and golfing hotels, all looking reverently down to the windswept, sand-sprinkled, treeless heath where the game was born.

Dominating the scene is the formidable club-house of the Royal and Ancient itself, the governing body of golf throughout the world. This is a stocky, many-chimneyed building at the end of the course, beside the Caddie Master's Office. It is seldom open to the public, so that inquisitive strangers must content themselves with looking rudely through its smoking-room window. But even this can be rewarding enough. The room looks exactly as it should, leathery and well worn, and in its big bay window a few club worthies are likely to be sitting

LITTLE PLOVER EGGS, CORAL SANDS, CLAIGAN, ISLE OF SKYE

around a table. Some will almost certainly have whisky glasses in their hands, all are sunk very memberly in their chairs; and as you go by, brazenly staring through the window, all those well-fed, ruddy, cautious Scottish faces will look back at you impassively, courteous but unsmiling, like off-duty priests in a vestry.

Probably most of us, though, when we think of a Scottish townsman, think of a Glaswegian; and this is proper, for more than half of all the people of Scotland live in Glasgow and its satellites. Not so long ago one went on to think almost automatically of slums, but today the civic reputation has spectacularly shifted. Economically the city may be limping, its shipyards eclipsed, its unemployment grim, but Glasgow's where the action is, young Scotsmen always say, Glasgow's The Scene. The old place is reborn, they claim, and it greets its visitors nowadays with a famous slogan of assurance, GLASGOW'S MILES BETTER! – hugely on public buildings, tirelessly in publicity brochures, inescapably on hoardings.

Physically it really has been transformed. The grim back-to-back slums of the Gorbals have vanished absolutely, to be replaced by the serried tower-blocks of urban renewal. The Queen's Dock, once jostling with the ships of all the oceans, has been filled in and turned into a futuristic exhibition centre. The river Clyde, which used to flow through the city smoky and rumbustious with traffic, has been prettied up with walks and gardens on its banks, and is more or less lifeless on its stream. The Victorian city centre is scoured of its grime, sooty old Central Station has been so thoroughly rejuvenated that it feels like a brand-new pastiche of its nineteenth-century self. Discos flourish in Glasgow back-streets, a converted church called the Cardinal's Folly

RIVER ORCHY, STRATHCLYDE

houses an expensive restaurant in its crypt, round and round like spanking toys go the brand-new yellow coaches of the Glasgow underground, surely the most engaging of all trains.

Intellectually, artistically, Glasgow is all alive. Both the Scottish Opera and the Scottish National Orchestra have their headquarters here, aficionados from all over the world come to play homage to Charles Mackintosh, Glasgow's great *fin-de-siècle* designer: his Willow Tea Rooms in Sauchiehall Street have been exquisitely restored, and with their glinting colours, their spindly high-backed furniture, their mirrors, their diamond windows and their air of goblin mystery, are like some Scottish jewel-house in a fairy tale. As to the new Burrell Collection, the pride of Glasgow museums, it has overtaken all lochs, castles, palaces and islands to be Scotland's No 1 tourist attraction: to house its collection of miscellaneous treasures, given to the city by a patriotic ship-owner, a long glassy building has been erected in a park, suggesting to me one of those canopies they sometimes place over archaeological sites or ancient ships – as though all those *objets d'art* had been piled up on the grass, and a great transparent shelter raised over them.

No doubt about it, in many ways Glasgow *is* miles better, and paradoxically in economic decline its civic stature has been newly revealed. The heavy city centre, for so long derided in its pomp and blackness, is seen in its new resplendence to be extremely fine, and even more striking are the nineteenth-century suburbs that spread away in crescent, square and boulevard to the west – well-kept, handsome suburbs, suburbs fit for a great city, centred upon the flamboyantly towered main buildings of the university, and furnished with delicatessens, Good Food Guide restaurants and unisex hairdressers.

And yet, and yet . . . for me the real fascination of the place lies still in the feisty, pawky and ribald character of the old Glasgow, which is city Scotland *in excelsis*. Fortunately time and trend have not destroyed it. Glasgow is an ancient city, far older than its Victorian climax, and its people seem immune to misfortune, cosmetic change or civic improvement. Wry, quick, funny, sceptical, your Glaswegian seems the same as ever, and it is his affectionate pride in his home town, more than any fancy development or publicity hype, that gives it some of the sensations of a city-state, complete and sovereign to itself –

> *When I've had a couple of drinks on a Saturday*
> *Glasgow belongs to me!*

The city docks have gone, the smoke is dispersed, expressways ring the city and stark high-rises punctuate it, but still as always the paper-boys are shouting 'Evening *Times*, Evening *Times*!' in the gloaming outside Central Station. Harry Lauder has long been in his grave, but Billy Connolly is now the hero of Glasgow audiences. Those towers of Gorbals may look antiseptic from a distance, but like their predecessor tenements they are scrawled with slogans vividly scurrilous or inflammatory. In the winter garden of the People's Palace they are still drinking morning tea beneath the tall and mournful palms. The figures surrounding the statue of Queen Victoria on Glasgow Green have one and all been mutilated by vandals, leaving them macabrely dismembered in homage around Her Majesty; but beyond them on the river bridges the lumbering buses blaze their message gamely across the water – GLASGOW'S MILES BETTER! GLASGOW'S MILES BETTER!

Only 45 miles to the east, linked to Glasgow by motorway through the spreading conurbations, stands Scotland's capital, Edinburgh, encouched beside its private mountain, Arthur's Seat, above the Firth of Forth. It is a copy-book capital, containing within its moderate limits (it is half the size of Glasgow) all the metropolitan prerequisites: a castle on a ridge, a royal palace, rich residential districts, an energetic commercial centre, its own seaport, memorials of a long enthralling history, and the remnants at least of that huddled anarchic quarter, essential to the balance of every great city, which owes allegiance to chaos rather than to order.

Not long ago I drove into Edinburgh during its celebrated international festival, the greatest of all Scottish occasions, and found it almost dizzily *en fête*. Flags flew wherever I looked, bands played, bright posters were stuck on every other wall, buskers strummed guitars or played Mozart quartets in underpasses, clowns clowned, jugglers juggled, every concert hall, art gallery, theatre, cinema, school, park, castle courtyard, palace garden, city square, sports centre, swimming bath, disused warehouse, abandoned shop, secularized chapel, railway station platform, hotel lobby, barracks, bankrupt garage and bus station seemed to be the venue for some sort of performance, exhibition, happening or public discussion. I drove into the city hilariously, now and then hooting my horn for fun; and when I parked outside my hotel somebody affixed a ticket to my windscreen – not a parking ticket, but a passionate gripe from a citizen ill-used by the city housing authorities, 'those monsters of tyranny and injustice'.

Anarchy? Certainly a healthy tinge of it. On Princes Street that day half a dozen side-shows were in full performance. An old-fashioned Socialist demagogue was haranguing the crowd from his soapbox. A

LOCH NAN UAMH, SOUND OF ARISAIG, HIGHLAND

AUCHNACREE, NEAR MONTROSE, TAYSIDE

man in full evening dress was singing 'On the Sunny Side of the Street' on the steps of the National Gallery. Two comedians dressed as ancient Egyptians were doing a comic act, and a tipsy old fellow in a kilt was dancing a reel to the music of a wind-up gramophone. All of a sudden amidst the hubbub two young toughs in shirt-sleeves struck up a bit of a fight, punching each other in a tentative way and exchanging high-pitched Scottish insults. Instantly all attention turned to them. The orator found his audience dwindling before his eyes, the ancient Egyptians were soon playing to an empty pavement, and swirling here and there across the pavement went the crowd, wavering and staggering with each exchange of blows. Through the mêlée, as it disappeared behind the Scott Memorial, I could see the fierce squabbling heads of the contestants, mouthing curses.

High above us the Old Town on its ridge seemed to watch the affray approvingly. It has always suggested to me the domain of chaos up there, shadowy in silhouette, spiky, tight-jammed around the cobbled grey street that leads a little crookedly from the castle to the royal palace. When I first went to Edinburgh, forty years ago, it was recognizably Auld Reekie, Old Smoky still; its buildings were blackened and hugger-mugger, its narrow courts were apparently half-derelict, small dirty windows looked down suspiciously from high gables, and it was a queer and pungent place indeed. Today it is bowdlerized, but still has a darkly atavistic feel. Architectural writers think of it as Romantic, but it seems brutal to me, and looking apprehensively towards that froward skyline, I find it easy even now to imagine the housewives throwing their slops into the streets from those high tenement windows, or spitting imprecations as the doomed Marquis of Montrose is led shackled down the Royal Mile to his execution.

But if the Old Town of Edinburgh is Instinct and Prejudice in stone, the New Town down below is all Pride and Reason. Its symmetrical eighteenth-century streets are spacious and logical, and look as though their inhabitants would not dream of spitting down a gutter, let alone upon a manacled marquis. The madcap frenzy of the festival only makes them seem the more restrained, and the glowering contrast of the medieval city high above, with its mighty flagstaffed castle top-heavy at one end, only seems to give them an extra equilibrium. The proximity of the New and Old Towns superbly reinforces Edinburgh's authority as a capital: you feel that at one and the same time, if need be, the elders of this city can consult the opinions of the great eighteenth-century Rationalists and summon the claymored clans from the Highlands.

But then Edinburgh is made for authority. Its situation above the Firth of Forth is marvellously authoritative, and it is full of the institutions of Establishment, government departments, universities, consulates, high courts, the Faculty of Actuaries, the huge and awful Scottish Office, the Records Office with a wind indicator on its façade, the Commission of Northern Lighthouses with a model lighthouse above its door. Here is the office of the Hong Kong Government, here the headquarters of the venerable *Scotsman* newspaper, here the Royal Bank of Scotland, with an equestrian figure in its courtyard who seems at first sight to be Napoleon but is really only the 4th Earl cf Hopetoun.

There is nothing provincial to it, though its population is less than half a million. It is made to be a capital. No railway station could be more metropolitan than Edinburgh's Waverley, in the very middle of the city, where the big sleek trains come in from London (the English trains, they call them), and where sometimes an unseen electric organ plays stirring and enormously amplified national airs. Edinburgh policemen can be very masterly, Edinburgh judges are infinitely judicial, and the very conception of sovereignty is embodied in the figures of those whole-hog patriots sometimes to be seen stalking these streets in full panoply of Scottishness – Harris tweed jackets, tartan kilts, deerhide sporrans, dirk-loaded knee-stockings, heavy leather shoes, fobwatches very likely, peppery moustaches, sharp blue eyes and all: looking a little self-conscious perhaps even here in the capital of their loyalties and longings, but still majestically in charge.

A few miles north of Edinburgh two of Europe's most famous bridges cross the Firth of Forth, side by side: the elaborate humped and cantilevered railway bridge (1890), all huge metal tubes and steel lattices, and the elegant road bridge (1964) with its slender towers and gently curving span. The firth grandly widens here, as it meets the open sea; tankers discharge at their moorings on the south side, warships lie in their dockyards on the north; in the distance is the haze of Edinburgh, and the hump of Arthur's Seat above the castle ridge; with those two immense works of engineering, that noble waterway, that splendid prospect, it is a place of terrific power.

Scotland is a country of power. It has no political power of its own, but it has power of many other kinds, to be felt most impressively here in the midlands. Here above all you may sense the latent power of the Scottish identity, totally different, totally separate from English sensibilities, and expressing itself in other images and aspirations; but here too in the centre of industrial strength and official purpose you are reminded always of Scotland's contribution to the power of Great

Britain. Scottish industry and ingenuity made this an engine-house of imperial expansion a century ago – they used to call Glasgow the British Empire's Second City; you have only to look at the memorials in Edinburgh's High Kirk to know how many Scotsmen went out to govern the far-flung possessions beneath the Union Flag (which originally included only the crosses of St George and St Andrew – St Patrick's was added later).

And everywhere there are tokens, proud and sad, of the part Scotsmen have played in the British wars – monuments, lists of casualties, cobwebby colours laid up in regimental museums, peacock-smart sentries at barrack gates, the beat of drums, the wail of the lone piper who, high on the castle ramparts, brings to a tear-jerking conclusion each evening of the Edinburgh Tattoo. The sadnesses have been terrible: even now, seventy years on, you may still see families thumbing through the registers in the national memorial to the dead of the First World War. The pride has been colossal: in the whole range of the military aesthetic there are no units to match the Scottish infantry regiments for cocky strut and spendour, and except perhaps for Napoleon's Old Guard none have ever beaten them for charisma.

More fundamental still to British power has been Scotland's place among the seas. The Royal Navy has always been a half-Scottish navy – in both world wars its main battle fleets were based on Scottish havens – and its presence is still ubiquitous. At an unsuspected quay on an unfrequented shore a naval tanker discharges its fuel. All down a dark loch are the towers and platforms of a torpedo range. On a headland far from anywhere a notice in old-school Admiralty language warns of bombardments – 'the inconvenience and delay caused to visitors is much regretted and will be kept to a minimum'. Through

FORVIE SANDS, NEWBURGH, GRAMPIAN

FORVIE SANDS

FORVIE SANDS

the drizzle a couple of minesweepers make for home, and down the waters of Gareloch, only twenty miles from Glasgow, you may catch a glimpse of one of the black nuclear submarines, *Repulse* or *Revenge, Sovereign* or *Superb*, on its way to prowl the seabeds.

It was at that place of power upon the Firth of Forth, where the two great bridges stand side by side, and where down countless generations kings and armies have crossed the water to conquest or sovereignty – it was there almost within sight of the Scottish capital that the British Empire reached a symbolic apogee of its strength. There, in November 1918, 5 battle-cruisers, 11 battleships, 10 cruisers and 50 torpedo boats of the German High Seas Fleet came out of a misty sea to Scotland, and surrendered themselves to the 20 admirals, the 90,000 men, the 370 warships of the Royal Navy assembled for their reception. It was the greatest capitulation in naval history. Two years later, as if in recognition of Scotland's place in the structure of power, the commander of the victorious fleet, Admiral Sir David Beatty, was elected Lord Rector of Edinburgh University.

THREE

Over the neck of Scotland, narrowed by its twin firths of Forth and Clyde, guarded by its twin citadels of Glasgow and Edinburgh, and you are unmistakably in the north – and not just in the north of Britain, either, but in the generic North, where the air is crisper, the light is paler, and for much of the year there is snow on a distant mountain. Aberdeen, the granite capital of the Scottish northlands, is further north than Labrador, and there is no land between the northern extremities of Scotland and the Pole itself.

In terrain as in meaning, there is nothing small about this country. If you are travelling from south to north of the British mainland, from the Straits of Dover to John O'Groats, when you cross the Forth Bridge outside Edinburgh you still have nearly half of your journey to go. Even as the crow, or the golden eagle flies, it is two hundred miles from Scotland's urban belt to its northern coast, while the north-western shores of the country are so fantastically complicated with islands and sea-inlets that you could sail for thousands of miles around them.

Not everything above the urban belt is mountain country – there is a rich coastal plain in the east, and in the far north-east, too, the hill country subsides into flatland. But it is from up here, in the magnificent, under-populated north, that the chief of all the Scottish images emanates: the image of the Highlands. This is the country of the clans, whose styles and customs have so enamoured the world, whose names ring so splendidly – Macleod and Macdonell, Cameron and Mackay – and some of whose chieftains still to this day live embattled, if only by

CALEDONIAN PINES, LOCH TULLA, STRATHCLYDE

tourists, in their castles. Here is that northern wasteland, one of the last great wildernesses of Europe, whose landscapes catch at the hearts of so many exiles, and excite the wanderlust of so many city people. Here the deer are stalked across the wide moors, here the salmon leap and the grouse fling themselves out of the heather. Pipes play up here, cabers are tossed at Highland Games, last enclaves of the Gaelic tongue fight for its survival.

There was a time when this empty country was not so empty, and many a now desolate hillside had its crofts, schools and chapels. In the eighteenth century the more unscrupulous Highland chieftains realized sheep to be more profitable tenants than human beings, in the nineteenth it dawned upon them that deer for the stalking were better than either. Many thousands of crofters were then evicted from their holdings, and shipped away to new Scotlands on the other side of the Atlantic. Small ruins everywhere are their only memorials; even their community records, as often as not, they took into exile with them, leaving their history blank.

So there is melancholy to the desertion of the Highlands, but there is undeniable grandeur too. This is an incomparably romantic landscape, like no other. For my tastes there is rather too much of it, one too many mountain, one too many loch; but then without a certain surfeit of desolation, some savage monotony, a wilderness would not be wilderness at all. As it is, the Scottish Highlands seem immense even beyond their limits. Much of the country is penetrable only on foot, and most of it is uninhabited still – how lonely the infrequent roads, single-tracked across the moors, and how perkily courageous the blue-and-white trains, snaking their routes between the mountains!

Sometimes it feels to me like one huge heaved hump of rock, white-

GLEN CANNICH, HIGHLAND

LOCH EIL AND BEN NEVIS, HIGHLAND

topped in the winter, heather-splashed in the warm – like an enormously magnified version of one of those isolated outcrops which sometimes protrude, all of a piece, out of deserts. But the Wagnerian homogeneity of the Highlands is relieved by a thousand grace-notes. Time and again you discover to your surprise some narrow sea-inlet cut sly and crooked in the side of the land, with a sudden sheen of Atlantic sunshine on it, and a fringe of surf. Around almost any corner you may expect to find a little lake, reedy around the edges, its surface scattered with water-lilies whose leaves, tilted in parallel by the wind, look like the sails of some elfin regatta. Peaty rivers splash tea-coloured out of their hills, and every now and then above the brooding massif there stands in thrilling contrast one of Scotland's more spectacular mountain shapes – the murderous silhouettes of the Cuillins on the Isle of Skye, the eccentric pillar of Suilven, the hefty hump-back of Ben Nevis, the highest mountain of the British islands. If you are lucky you may see an eagle riding the wind, or spot red deer on a skyline; there are foxes about, and brown hares, and pine martens, and glaring at you undetected from some crevice or coppice may be the implacable yellow eyes of a wild cat . . .

Many people, urban people especially perhaps, find these superb prospects calming and uplifting. I am moved by them in another way, for I find them disturbingly at odds, out of scale, lacking the harmony and proportion that the Chinese look for in their ideal landscapes. Either way, exalting or perturbing, they make for a tremendously demanding environment, where in the past only the toughest could survive. There are no cities in the Scottish Highlands, and very few towns: life is concentrated upon a handful of roadside villages. There you may still meet the courteous, sensitive and elusive Highlander of

THE CUILLIN HILLS, ISLE OF SKYE

PETER MACLEOD, DUNTULM, ISLE OF SKYE

legend. In all the six million acres of the Highland mainland there are less than 200,000 people, and even among them your true Highlander is often overwhelmed by newcomers. For all his legendary resilience and his military traditions, his is a fragile presence. Across these thin soils, among these grand inhospitable ranges, he seems to move airily – proud of his country, but somehow detached from it, wary of it perhaps, as though life has always been too hard up there, history too unreliable, to encourage the setting down of certainties.

Startlingly up the eastern shore runs Scotland's Oil Coast – startling because the fizz and gleam of it, the strange artifacts and gaudy colours, the cosmopolitan push, the noise, the rush and violent energy all seem at first sight incongruous to the setting. The east coast is lowland country, but the forbidding Grampian Mountains are no more than forty miles inland, and in an easy hour you can travel from the wildest of empty moorlands to Dyce airport by the sea, where helicopters take off night and day for the rigs of the North Sea oilfields.

People of many nationalities extract the oil from Scotland's waters, and all Britain shares the profits, but it is of course upon Scotland that the full blast of the industry has fallen. Indirectly the benefits of oil have been distributed through every social, political, commercial, financial, industrial and academic artery of Scotland; here on the coast of Aberdeen their effect has been immediate. Here the great international companies have established themselves, and from here the distant rigs are serviced and maintained. Vast sums of oil money are channelled through the banks of Aberdeen, spin-off industries of a hundred kinds have come into being. It says much about the northern character that the impact of this astonishing bonanza has been so imperturbably absorbed.

Of course it is apparent – in the quickened and invigorated pace of things, in a general sense of diffused prosperity, in big American cars around the place, and smart new businessmen's hotels, in strangely bulbous and knobbly oil-boats moored in old fishing harbours, in the monstrous oil-rigs themselves sometimes to be seen towed past out at sea. Aberdeen is full of the agencies and repercussions of oil, from night clubs to conglomerate offices, from the coming and going of tenders and tankers to new research projects in university laboratories. Dyce, the busiest helicopter port in Europe, is as explicit an illustration as you could find of oil's furious energy, so relentless is the whirring and roaring of those machines, so ceaseless the transit of oil workers from every corner of the world, so jam-packed are the car parks, so strangely evocative the names of the sea-rigs on the destination boards – Active King, Auk, Wimpey Sea-Fox, Cormorant . . .

Yet along this staunch and canny coastline nothing essential seems to have changed. People are not extravagantly dressed. They count their change just as carefully in the shops, they inspect the menu prices just as thriftily in the restaurants. I asked a woman once if everybody was the better off for the arrival of oil. 'You wouldna know it,' she said, and she was right – from appearances at least, you wouldna. Aberdeen itself, now one of the principal oil cities of the world, cautiously keeps to itself the effects of its windfall, and prepares for its eventual end – as its citizens love saying, you must take care of the future, for 'the future willna take car o' itself'. Aberdeen has always been a spectacular place in its way, the Granite City of the north, strong, stoic, self-sufficient, and its exotic new functions have certainly not gone to its head. The

PAPS OF JURA FROM KNAPDALE, STRATHCLYDE

GLEN COE, HIGHLAND

LOCH MORLICH, CAIRNGORMS, HIGHLAND

handsome old streets look as sedate, as provincially respectable as ever. The harbour, though littered with those queer oil craft as by an infiltration from outer space, is still the archetypal Scottish fishing port, all masts, oil-skins and rich dialect, all slither and wooden crates in the half-light of the dawn. There is no frenzy to this boom town, which remains deliberate, law-abiding and taciturn, in the old Scots way.

Is there another city in the world, I wonder, which would have taken the whirlwind of oil so calmly in its stride? It is as though Aberdeen has simply accepted its good fortune, put the money under its mattress and continued as before. This is no place for silly ostentation, and if others may find these responses a little lacking in panache, Aberdonians do not care. On the walls of Marischal College in this city there is an inscribed stone whose medieval text perfectly expresses the municipal attitude. 'THEY HAIF SAID', announces this gnomic declaration, and goes on to answer itself very authentically: 'QUHAT SAY THEY? LAT THAME SAY'.

Oil is transient bonanza, as the Aberdonians know so well. A more permanent mainstay of the north is whisky – *uisge beatha* in the Gaelic, meaning water of life. Scotch whisky is the distillation of Scotland itself: truly, as the Colonel said, the wine of the country. They make it in one kind or another in many parts of Scotland, in Lowlands as in Highlands, at Ladyburn far in the south, at Pulteney in the extreme north, in Orkney and the Inner Hebrides, where it smells of the island peat. But the most famous source of all is Speyside, between the Grampians and the sea. Through this rolling hilly country the publicists of the industry have laid out the Malt Whisky Trail, a Scottish equivalent of the Wine Routes in Burgundy or California, which takes its pilgrims

meandering up the valley of the Spey to the places where pure malt whisky is made. The rules of its production are strict: it must be made of Highland barley dried over peat fires, it must be watered with streams that have run through peat over red granite, it must be distilled in pot-vats of particular shape and stored in old oak barrels – processes all absolutely essential, they say, to the unmistakable taste of Speyside.

The Whisky Trail is not much like those wine routes. The hills of Speyside give no inkling of the priceless liquors they secrete. They are modest and welcoming hills, spiced with woodlands, overlooked by moors, and the burns that run through them are undramatic. There is nothing to tell you as you drive up from the coast that this is the home of Glenfiddich and Glenfarcas, Tamdhu and The Glenlivet, names which give a warm glow to connoisseurs in every corner of the world. The small towns of Speyside look to the stranger more like mill towns than bottling towns, producing tweeds or wholemeal flour rather than the water of life.

Yet there they are, the world-celebrated distilleries, often clenched narrowly within their particular stretch of valley, beside their own indispensable stream. They look very private, rather swart sometimes with their chimneys and their severe-looking yards, except for those which have rearranged themselves for the tourists with gardened car parks and gift shops. Nor do they seem, from the outside, very busy – one or two of them actually look abandoned, and others give an impression of decidedly leisurely production. But they are indisputably the Real Thing, the objects of many a distant devotion, the targets of many a plotted takeover. Speyside is the Côte d'Or of Scotland. As Belloc might have said, 'I don't remember the name of the village, I

STOB NAN CABER, GLENCOE, HIGHLAND

TIGERTON, TAYSIDE

don't remember the name of the girl, but the whisky was Speyside . . .'

I have disliked whisky all my life, but wandering along that Trail one day, and stopping to eat my corned beef sandwich at the famous distilling centre of Dufftown, I felt it my duty to try once more. I went to a nearby pub and asked for a dram of the local water of life, to drink with my victuals on a bench in the square outside. The barmaid looked at me quizzically. 'I'm not sure the law allows it. But seeing as you're a visitor . . .' And accepting my plastic mug, she poured into it a full measure of malk whisky – one of the very best, she said, from a distillery just down the road. I concealed it inside my open bag as I left the inn, and turning to the door I saw her winking at me conspiratorially, as though I had poached a salmon.

No Speyside constable intervened. No Revenue man expostulated. There in the square I started on my sandwich, and when I thought my thirst had been sufficiently stimulated, I took a cautious swig of the whisky. Dear God, it was nectar! Was it the freshness of it, was it the fact that I was drinking it upon a bench beneath the clock in Dufftown square, was it that wink from the barmaid, was it just the legendary presence of Speyside all around? Whatever it was, whisky had never tasted like that before, and perhaps never will again. I may forget the place, I may forget the corned beef sandwich, but I shall never forget the Balvenie!

Diagonally across the northlands runs the Great Glen, a string of lakes and declivities which, linked by the nineteenth-century Caledonian Canal, connects the North Sea with the Atlantic. It is lined with bare hills, thickly patched with conifer woods, and is sometimes still traversed by a yacht or a fishing boat on its way from one sea to the

NEAR LOCH CLUANIE, HIGHLAND

other. But it is famous to the world chiefly because of its deepest and longest lake, Loch Ness, where the most celebrated of contemporary chimeras does or does not live.

I went there once, like many another, specifically to contemplate the mystery, and wanting it to be true: for the monster of Loch Ness seems to me to represent the other side of life, the side we cannot see – and what could be bleaker than to discover, one day, that there *is* no other side? So I chose a properly suggestive morning, blowy and overcast, and drove to the loch from Inverness. The road on its northern side is habitually packed with traffic, but the road along the southern shore is inexplicably neglected – only a forestry centre, a few scattered houses and the village of Dores lie upon it, and few tourists use it. That was the way I chose, and parking my car on the very edge of the loch, I looked expectantly out across its waters.

Infinitely grey, infinitely silent lay Loch Ness that day. On the other side I could see the traffic hastening by, but I could hear nothing of it. On my side hardly a car passed. The surface of the lake, ruffled by a constant wind, was blotched with dark patches here and there, so that like everyone else every few minutes I seemed to see, until the light changed or the wind momentarily slackened, a black head swimming, an eel-like loop of neck, or just the wake of something on the move. The longer I stared the more I saw these things, and the more visionary, the less frivolous, I felt the whole conception of the Loch Ness monster to be. And in these responses, I was presently to find, I was not alone.

A young forester walked by, and I asked him if he had ever seen the creature of the loch. He did not smile at the question. He had lived there always, he said, but he had not seen it yet. For him though its

STRATH CONON, HIGHLAND

existence or non-existence was not important, for he interpreted it as a didactic figure of faith. 'It teaches us to believe in something that we canna see – you understand me?' He thought a great deal about the matter, he told me, and often looked out there on the half-chance of seeing the monster. I said I seemed to see it every five minutes, but again he did not laugh. 'Well, before you go home,' he said meaning-fully, looking me straight in the eye, 'I hope you see it *truly* . . .'

At his suggestion I called upon a lady of Dores who has, on the other hand, seen the creature many times, and is familiar with the bubbling and heaving of waters that it is said to leave behind – the stretch of loch between Dores and the castle of Urquhart, she told me, was well known to be the animal's pleasure-ground. Well known? Why cer-tainly, for once she had decided I was not there to mock, she discussed the subject with an air of proud certainty, like one who has experi-enced wonders for herself. She was *enthusiastic* about it, in the religious sense, like a born-again Christian. She assured me that nearly every-one around there knew the monster existed, however reluctant they were to talk about it to outsiders, and she made it all sound at once everyday and profoundly arcane: a fact of life or of conviction cherished in private by a whole community, defying all that publicity, science, tourism and tomfoolery could do. 'I do hope I see it,' I said. 'I hope you do,' she said very seriously, like the forester before her, as if to say that indeed I might, if Providence were kind, be admitted to that inner knowledge of the loch.

When I left her I sat again at the water's edge. Could it be, I won-dered, that the Loch Ness monster was something altogether mystical or allegorical, a purely imaginary shadow on the lake, an idea, passed down from generation to generation among these people? Or were

LOCH LOCHY, HIGHLAND

they the possessors of some immemorial intuition, unformulated perhaps even in their own consciousness, but embodied in the timeless image of that water-creature? I stared and stared, and thought and thought; but though I willed all my subconscious power to reveal to me the meaning of the loch, I never did see it materialize, even in hallucination, out of those cold and haunted waters.

Scattered through the Highlands, sheltered in glens or reckless on the shores of lakes, many great houses stand – castles big and small, shooting lodges and a dizzy plethora of Victorian Gothic mansions. Though many of them are in ruins now, and few are private homes any more, set against the stern immensity of the setting they seem to speak reassuringly of security, warm welcomes and good living.

Especially perhaps good living, which has always been part of the Scottish style. Plentiful victuals, firelit inns, pipes lit and feet on the table – all this has traditionally been part of life as of literature (for where would a Burns be without a dram, or a Scott without a haunch of venison?). Elsewhere in the world the Scottish cuisine may be generally thought of as consisting entirely of haggis and chips, but actually at its best it can be magnificent; and so it ought to be, for the very substance of the country suggests it – the heathery fragrant moors, the dark mysterious lochs, the deep cold waters of the surrounding seas, the tumble of salmon streams, the high frosty airs through which, distantly silhouetted on moorland ridges, future haunches of venison graze and rut.

The heyday of well-heeled Scottish comfort was unquestionably the nineteenth century, when the Victorian fashion for all things

LOCH QUOICH, HIGHLAND

LOCH CRERAN, STRATHCLYDE

GLEN QUOICH FOREST, HIGHLAND

Caledonian gave a new impetus to hospitality, and the grand country house was at its apogee. Glistening lay the salmon in their silver dishes then, richly sizzled the roasting deer, fresh were the eels from Loch Tay or the turbot from St Abbs, hung to a nicety was the noble grouse! Few can live like that in Scotland now – the Queen and her family in their several Scottish homes, some dukes and marquises in their ancestral seats, a few industrialists and pop stars in their country retreats – but fortunately for us many of those old mansions have now been turned into hotels, sometimes by family inheritors, sometimes by canny entrepreneurs. To spend a night in one of these is to experience a kind of reincarnation, if only in pastiche, of Scottish hedonism a century ago.

Here stands such a house now conveniently beside the road. It is surrounded by rhododendron bushes and conifers, and backed by a small lake ornamentally bridged. A fairly bumpy drive deposits us beneath a heavy *porte-cochère* beside an iron-studded front door. From the principal turret of Aberlochly House a large flag flies, possibly the rampant lion of Scotland, more probably a family ensign; lavishly strewn about its walls are crests, gargoyles and chiselled mottoes. There may be a croquet lawn, there is very likely a dalliance where Princess Alexandra, on her well-remembered visit to Aberlochly with the future Edward VII, liked to sit in the sun between outings.

Inside an air of slightly tenuous grandeur prevails. All the statutory tokens of country-house living are there in abundance: open fires with parallel sofas, piles of *Country Life* or *The Field*, rather too many exquisitely arranged flowers, heads of stags shot by late baronial owners, pictures of gigantic fish caught by eminent guests, huge books of

LICHEN ON PINE BARK, LOCH MAREE, HIGHLAND

coloured plates illustrating Scottish castles and landscapes, crested albums commemorating the visit of the future King Edward VII in 1895. Our food is all we expect it to be – rich, and bold, and fresh, and Scottish. Our whisky is Speyside malt, of course, our wine is probably not from the supermarket. The atmosphere of Aberlochly is plush and genial. The proprietor, whether he be an actual laird making the best of things, or a pretend laird capitalizing upon legendary delights, is likely to move among his guests in a manner almost excessively hostly, castellan and considerate.

So we discover, as in a time-warp, the traditional comforts of Scotland, captured here in the ample refinement of its most comfortable period and most privileged class. Behind the house the woodlands of the old estate rise to the distant deer-forests, and above the lake, beyond the somewhat tumbledown ha-ha, flocks of Canada geese honk and wheel in the evening.

Where are the Gaels, the old champions of the north? Where can their language be heard? You must travel far into these northlands if you pine for the Celtic heritage, for over the centuries its language has been compressed ever further into the remote north-west, and out into the islands of the Atlantic. A century ago there were more than a quarter of a million Gaelic-speakers in Scotland; today there are less than 80,000 – perhaps one in 70 of the population – and except for migrants in the great cities they are overwhelmingly in the north-west. The stranger journeying northwards from the English border may detect no living sign of the language until, dropping down through Braemor Forest

CLACCAN, NORTH UIST, OUTER HEBRIDES

high on the Ross coast, he finds at the entrance to the seaside town of Ullapool its name announced in Gaelic.

Alas, that is probably all the Gaelic he will find in the little town – founded as a fishing port in 1788, in a very Gaelic part of Scotland, and the base of a fishing fleet still, but full of caravans, craft shops, tourists and English accents. Did nobody speak Gaelic there any more, I once asked a woman at a petrol station? 'A few of the locals do,' she said dismissively, 'but they disappear in the summer' – and instantly I was reminded of Dr Johnson, who declared Gaelic to be 'the rude speech of a barbarous people who had few thoughts to express'. I asked at the post office, the police station and two hotels how to spell the town in Gaelic, and nobody knew. A handful of house names and self-conscious shop signs, perhaps a token dictionary in a bookshop, ULLAPUL disregarded at the town entrance – that's about the measure of Ullapool's Gaelicness.

Out in the Atlantic isles Gaelic still gallantly holds its own, and it is taught in the schools of the west; but here on the coast of the Highlands the language has almost fallen into silence, and in most other parts of the country, for all the efforts of its indefatigable lovers, you will never hear it spoken. Town names there are to be found in their original forms only on Gaelic-language maps. Where is Glasche? Where is Dun Eideann? How would you travel from Dundeagh to Abaireadhain? They are Glasgow and Edinburgh to all the world now, and the road runs north from Dundee to Aberdeen. Alas, it may be that before another couple of generations have passed even the Gaelic maps will be out of print, and Scottish Gaelic will have joined its semantic fellow-ghosts, Cornish, Manx and the lost Celtic tongues of the European

LOCH MULLARDOCH, HIGHLAND

continent, in the limbo of phantom languages.

Yet often enough, as you drive through the north-west mainland of Scotland, you will come by chance across a Gaelic programme on FM radio. Whenever this happens to me it gives me a frisson of excitement. Utterly dry those ancient syllables sound, utterly flint-like, hanging on the clear air without a breath of interference or a crackle of static. Then it does not sound like a dying language at all, but seems to be speaking to me still out of the lofty confidence of its prime.

RIVER HELMSDALE, SUTHERLAND

BLACK MOUNT, RANNOCH MOOR, STRATHCLYDE

FOUR

Looking out of my hotel window one morning at Lochinver, on the far north-western Assynt coast, where the bald sugar-loaf of Suilven rises so peculiarly above the sea, I saw in the water of the harbour below three swimming heads, contentedly lolling in the water, and sometimes sidling up to the pier where the local fishing boats were moored. At first I thought they were dogs, then bald elderly men, and finally I realized that they were seals. Nobody took the slightest notice of them, not the fishermen on the pier, not the truck-drivers, not the boys with their bikes, not the miscellaneous local loungers, certainly not the big seagulls forever tugging at discarded bits of fish or half-dismembered eels on the seaweedy pebbles below me. When I mentioned them to the waitress in the dining-room at breakfast she said, 'Oh yes, they're always there, like a lot of beggars . . .'

Nowhere in Scotland are you more than forty miles from the sea. The cities of Scotland are nearly all seaports, and around the long coastline, clear-cut in the east, crazily indented and islanded in the west, are scattered innumerable lesser harbours, their backs to the high ground, their fronts to the water. Of all the fish that is landed in Great Britain, 60 per cent is landed in Scotland, almost all of it in Scottish boats – every day the radio broadcasts the fish prices, and reports the amounts landed of hake or cod, plaice or monkfish. Scottish life is ineradicably permeated with matters of the sea. Sea-smells, sea-sounds, sea-sights, sea-creatures, sea-memories, sea-talk – all these are part of the very feel of the country: no wonder the residents of

MORAR, HIGHLAND

118

Lochinver hardly notice those mammals in the harbour.

Scotland often reminds me of Yugoslavia, another country with a long island-strewn coastline. There the ships are moving always beneath the white limestone ridge of the *karst*; here they come and go from their fiords in the lee of the bare mountains. Ships are always on the move in Scotland. Ferries steam out to the isles, freighters sail lordly beneath bridges, those esoteric oil craft scurry about Aberdeen, submarines sneak into secluded bases, fishing boats are crammed into the stony harbours of the east, factory ships from Eastern Europe stand waiting for mackerel off Ullapool, far out at sea you may see the trawlers dipping and plunging in their icy waters.

Very often too, crossing a ridge or rounding a bend, you come across an isolated fishing station, miles from almost anywhere, with a couple of boats moored beside its pier, a warehouse and a truck waiting to whisk the fish away to Inverness, Aberdeen or Glasgow. It is quite likely to look brand new, having been revivified lately with money from the European Common Market. On a still day, when the water of the sea-loch is mirror-like and the silent hills are reflected all about, and the only sounds, perhaps, are the chug of a generator and an occasional shout or burst of laughter, such an unexpected little port can be wonderfully suggestive – like some secret haven of skulduggery, I always think, hidden away from the coastguards.

Tradition has always played a powerful part in the sea-affairs of Scotland – tradition and plain pride. Pride was famously strong at Clydebank, the river town outside Glasgow in whose yards so many of the world's greatest liners and warships were built, but which is now hardly more than an industrial backwater. I stopped there one day outside the former yards of John Brown, once the most famous of all

LOCHALINE, HIGHLAND

LOCH MEADIE, HIGHLAND

the world's shipbuilders, and asked a passing woman if this really was the place where the *Queen Mary* was launched. 'The very place,' she said, and she looked with true and sad affection towards the empty slipway where, nearly fifty years before, the hull of the great liner had loomed over the street. It was as though she were looking at an old family house, or remembering triumphs of her own lost youth – 'Great days,' she said, 'happy days!'

And the tradition of a thousand years seemed to be embodied in the person of an elderly inshore fisherman I watched one sunny morning bringing his boat single-handed into the harbour of St Andrews. All the sea-skill of the ages informed him, I thought, as steering his boat with one hand he cleansed it with the other of all the crabs' legs, starfish, mangled bits of lobster and miscellaneous muck that had accrued upon its deck – a deft swoosh of the bucket, the handiest swish of a brush, and swinging his boat around as neat as could be, there he was tied up safe and snug at the quayside. (I asked him how long he had been out. He looked up at me severely through his steel-rimmed spectacles, and responded with a very Scottish counter-question. *'Have you any particular reason for wanting to know?'*)

There was nothing very traditional, though, about the fishing port at Lochinver, where those seals were. From my window I could watch all its activities – the coming and going of the boats, the rumbling arrival of the huge refrigerator trucks, the bright lights shining inside the warehouse, the flickering TV sets in the wheelhouses of off-duty boats. Visitors might be disappointed, if they came hoping for old-fashioned Scottish seamen, God-fearing and soft-spoken, devoted to myths and ancient superstitions of the sea. Some unusually colourful and obscene graffiti, I found, had been scrawled upon the walls of the Lochinver

IONA ISLAND

DURNESS, HIGHLAND

ABHAINN CEANN, LOCH AINORT, ISLE OF SKYE

fish-shed; and when the boats came in from sea, their crews first went next door for a quick drink at the bar, and then, jumping noisily into their cars, whooshed off clean across Scotland to Inverness, eighty miles away, where nearly all of them resided.

However far you travel up the mainland of Scotland – right the way to Cape Wrath and John O'Groats, where the two seas meet, away to the last peninsula of the west – always further still lie the islands. Sometimes you hardly know they are islands, so close do they lie inshore, and their hills seem merely extensions of the mainland ridges. Sometimes on the contrary they look a very apotheosis of islandness, humped eerie rocks far out at sea, white with swarming seabirds, or grey-clad with seamen's houses around a harbour. And sometimes they lie so far beyond the horizon that you cannot see them at all – Shetland on a level with Bergen or Helsinki; Rockall, the last barren outpost of the west, three hundred miles out in the Atlantic. Some of the Scottish islands have thriving populations, some are uninhabited. Some are flat, some are mountainous. Some are warmed by the Gulf Stream, some are almost Arctically uncompromising, some make tweeds or malt whisky, some make nothing at all. A few of them are famous everywhere in the world, most of them you can hardly discover on a large-scale map.

The islands provide a kind of harum-scarum cadenza to the theme of Scotland, for they are dizzily rich in exception and surprise, contrast and ambiguity. Even their names sound surrealist – Muck and Eigg and Staffa, Rhum and Mull, Ghiga, Hoy, Mingulay and the dream-like Summer Isles! They are as varied in character as in physical kind, and often seem, even now, like little kingdoms of their own. Arran may be the favourite destination of day-trips from Glasgow, but it is like a self-contained microcosm of Scotland as a whole – lowland, highland and seashore all within its narrow circuit. Iona, where St Columba established Christianity fourteen centuries ago, may be hardly a stone's throw from Mull but is like a separate holy world. South Uist, Eriskay and Barra have never given up their Catholic faith. On Skye for seven hundred years the chiefs of the MacLeods have lived like petty monarchs at Dunvegan, the oldest inhabited castle in Britain.

They can be formidably esoteric. In the islands of the west there is a Celtic air of withdrawal. In the islands of the north, Scandinavia and the Baltic seem always close, and the legacies of the Norsemen are everywhere. You can all but see the longboats of the sagas sailing across Orkney's eerie Scapa Flow, and the cathedral of St Magnus at Kirkwall, a mile or two away, is like a hefty fortress-church, a sacred bastion of the north. Up here the Norsemen ruled for generations, impervious to the power of the Scottish kings, and indeed extending their own empire far down into Scotland itself; and to this day in the streets of Stromness or Kirkwall you may imagine the authority of Earl Magnus or Earl Haakon all around you, and see in the faces of amiable passers-by the fierce hawked features of the galley men.

As for Shetland, still further to the north, it hardly feels like Scotland at all. The oil industry has fallen upon this archipelago like a stroke of destiny, but still the Shetland Islands feel astonishingly separate and idiosyncratic. There are more than a hundred of them, nearly all uninhabited. Their winds have been known to blow at 177 mph, they are so austerely treeless that their own people call them generically 'The Old Rock', and almost everything about them is their own. There are Shetland ponies, Shetland sheep, Shetland dogs, Shetland superstitions,

JOHN MACLEOD, 29TH CHIEF OF CLAN MACLEOD, DUNVEGAN CASTLE, ISLE OF SKYE

CATH KEENEY AND ANDREW, LARGIBEG, ISLE OF ARRAN

BORGIE, NEAR TONGUE, SUTHERLAND

Shetland sausages, Shetland shawls, and a Shetland dialect derived partly from Lowland Scottish, but partly from Norn, the ancestor of Norwegian. Lerwick, the capital, began as a German trading settlement in the fifteenth century, and its life still sometimes feels Hanseatic, or perhaps Ibsenite. In the long pale summer night, the Simmer Dim when it never gets dark, up there among those peat-black landscapes of Shetland, mysteriously flickering sometimes with the flashes of Aurora Borealis, sometimes with the lights of tankers, aircraft or oil-camps, you feel a long, long way from Edinburgh.

'Still in my dreams,' says the old song, 'I see the Hebrides', but there is far more to the Scottish isles than sweet nostalgia. Without them Scotland would not be Scotland; without their inescapable shapes offshore, the ferries perpetually nosing through their straits and inlets, the legends that reach us out of their remote and stormy pasts, and the ever magnetic knowledge of their presence, always out there, always a little further on.

A fine big ferry sails from Ullapool to the island of Lewis, in the Outer Hebrides. On it, as I sailed out one drizzly evening past the isolated crofts of Coigach, I ate absolutely the best fish and chips of my life – 'ONE FUSH!' the man called out from the serving counter when it was ready, and it had been caught that morning, and was teamed with potatoes fried with a most delicate dryness. Nearly everyone on board seemed to be islanders going home – very Scottish, *extremely* Scottish people, more than one the spitting image of King James VI. They drank moderately at the bar, they called trumps gently at the card schools that sprang up around the saloons, they gazed dreamily out of the windows, and they discreetly looked the other way when from the

COIGACH, HIGHLAND

recesses of my bag I pulled a half-bottle of Chablis to drink with my magnificent meal.

I had been to most of the big Scottish islands at one time or another – to Skye and Mull off the western shore, to the spare and thrilling Orkneys, to the Shetlands. Now I was going to the westernmost of them all, the westernmost part of Scotland, the westernmost part of Britain, the north-western extremity, no less, of the European continent. Lewis is joined to Harris, where the tweed is made, and the whole is called the Long Island. I had never been there before, but it sounded the most traditional of all the islands, the most wet and windswept, the most Gaelic, above all the most Godly – in short, like my fellow-passengers on the ferry, the most absolutely Scottish of all; so I arranged that my first morning there should be the morning of the Sabbath.

Stornoway – Steornabagh to Gaelic-speakers – is the capital and chief town of the Long Island, and is a substantial port with two harbours, lots of churches, several Pakistani shopkeepers and a nineteenth-century castle, now a technical college, dominating everything from a wooded prominence. It was soon after nine when I sauntered out from my hotel into this pleasant-looking place – soon after nine on a powerfully blustery Sunday morning. I found it, as I had rather hoped, absolutely stone-cold dead. Down at the harbour my ferry of the night before still lay sleeping at the quay, being forbidden to sail on Sundays, and around the corner the fishing boats too were utterly deserted. No children played in the public playground – it was not allowed – and it was no good trying to use the public lavatories, for they were locked. The waterfront disco looked positively battened down against the very suggestion that it might open for business, the

JIM CORBETT, KINLOCH SPELVE, MULL

138

LOCH BLASHAVAL, NORTH UIST, OUTER HEBRIDES

Sunday papers would not arrive until tomorrow, and it felt as though the entire community was planning to stay behind locked doors all day, repenting.

But come mid-morning, and lo, the town of Stornoway was brought gloriously to life! It was like spring after winter! Out of those doors the populace poured, into those silent streets crowded the cars, and suddenly the place was alive with eager bustle. Not the grey pinched stares I had expected, but friendly faces greeted me along the pavements, and from all corners laughing families made their way to worship. Who needed recreation grounds, I began to think, when church seemed so much fun? The dark-suited elders of the separate persuasions, Free Church here, Church of Scotland there, stood at their respective doors wreathed in inviting smiles, like car salesmen or rival cinema commissionaires, and gestured me to join their devotions.

But no, I loitered at an agnostic distance from those houses of God, listening to the music. From one church came the lusty tones of an English hymn, from another something much more suggestive – the chanting of metrical psalms in Gaelic, an old lament, almost a wail, almost tragic. And with this ancient music in my ears, I drove out of town into the peaty, windy, wet and heroic presence of Lewis – which is mostly flat bogland, speckled with the shanties of the peat-cutters, but which rises in the south into high and treeless moor.

I say heroic, because the mere fact of living on Lewis seems to me a courageous act – dying too, for never was there a braver burial ground than the wind-racked, salt-sprayed, rain-soaked cemetery that lies on a ridge just outside Stornoway, full of dead seamen and triumphantly surveying, this way and that, the tumultuous waters of the west. Almost everything in Lewis smacks of heroism. The straggling untidy

BRENISH, LEWIS, OUTER HEBRIDES

FROM EAVAL, NORTH UIST, OUTER HEBRIDES

villages look heroically long-suffering. The cottages, boats often in their gardens, look heroically robust. The survival of the Gaelic tongue, here tenaciously hanging on, is certainly heroic. The people themselves, bent against the Atlantic gales, seem heroes every one. 'You must all be heroes,' I remarked to a very old man heaving two brimming buckets of water through his garden. The wind was whistling through his shirtsleeves, flapping his trousers and blowing his dog's hair inside-out. 'Aye, but ye get used to the feeling,' he said, staggering through the door of his house.

Stocky, heavy-shouldered, stooped with his burden, he looked rather as though he had come out of the ground, like a hobbit, and the authentic Black House of the Outer Hebrides, a thatched mound-like structure of huge rough stones, really was as much like a lair as a residence. A few examples survive, most of them in ruins, and look to me as though they have been heaved up from underground, rather than deposited on the surface of the ground. They suit the landscape wonderfully. Though the islanders of Lewis are as kind and friendly a people as you could hope to meet, they do undeniably live strangely, in a strange place.

Strange by any standards is the celebrated stone circle of Callanish, one of the greatest of neolithic monuments, which stands in a field bathed very often, at least to my eyes, in a pale, slightly orange glow that seems to issue from the waters of the sea-loch beyond. Sometimes embedded in the stones of such circles one may fancy elements of primeval warmth, but if you lay your cheek against the central monolith of Callanish, hoping for some immemorially lichenous response, you will find it entirely cold and lifeless: and this makes the place feel

HUSINISH, NORTH HARRIS, OUTER HEBRIDES

CALLANISH, LEWIS, OUTER HEBRIDES

CALLANISH, LEWIS

queerer still, suggesting as it does that no human emotion has ever warmed those boulders.

Then there is the strangeness of the western light, which sometimes makes the sea look a leaden silvery colour, like mercury, and the strangeness of the black peat-bogs, and the strange allure of the Lewis seashore, with its myriad small treeless peninsulas, its salt-marshes, its desolate offshore islets – Rona and the Shiants, the Flannan Isles, Mealista. They used to think that a race of dwarfs inhabited Pigmies Island, and every year the men of northern Lewis sail over to the island of Slisgeir to kill the guga – young gannets, since time beyond memory a favourite local delicacy.

And so as in fantasy I made my way that day to the very top of the island, the very last north-western extremity of Scotland, with no land between it and the Pole to the north, Canada to the west. A lighthouse stands up there at the Butt of Lewis, and an immense foghorn on top of a pillar, labelled unnecessarily NOISE. Beyond it all is rock, foam, tide, wind, waste, mist, ebb and flow, hidden shoal, ice, prowling submarines, seals, guga, fog, echo, howl, summer dim and winter darkness. It is the end of a road if ever there was one, and just as we have arrived there now at the end of a literary traverse through Scotland, so I found myself there then at the end of an actual journey.

It was a raging, whistling, cruel day. I went as close as I dared to the edge of the precipitous rock, blown all about by the tremendous wind, the salt stinging my lips, the crazy seabirds whirling and shrieking overhead: and looking over the lip of it, I saw in a declivity below me two spherical greenish objects, huddled together in the earth. I could get no closer to them. The wind threatened to pluck me away. For the

CALLANISH, LEWIS

GIGHA ISLAND FROM KINTYRE

THE CUILLINS AND LOCH SCAVAIG, ISLE OF SKYE

life of me I could not make out what they were. Guga eggs? Snakes' eggs? Bombs? Balls from some ancient Hebridean game? Fungi? Huge gemstones? Fruits? Fetishes?

The wind blew. The gulls shrieked. The sign said NOISE. Regaining my car and with difficulty opening its door against the gale, I retreated from heroic, bewildering, indefatigable and tantalizing Scotland.

FINIS

I can hardly conclude with unidentified spheres on a windswept headland – Scotland demands some less whimsical finale. Let me instead take you south again, back across the empty Highlands, between the great cities of the centre, through the valleys of the south until we stand where we started, almost on the English border.

Outside the little weaving town of Langholm a hill looks towards England, and on it are two monuments. Half-way up, along a winding narrow road, stands a memorial lately erected to Hugh MacDiarmid, that gritty, mischievous but lyrical *genius loci*. It is a large oblong slab of bronze and steel, the shape of an open book, cut through as in filigree with a multitude of images – birds, a rainstorm, sheaves of corn, a pipe, and slyly in one corner a silhouetted portrait of the poet. The thing is implanted directly into the turf, and it looks back at you cheerfully, perhaps a little restlessly, with churned mud all around its feet.

Beyond it on the summit of the hill, often half-veiled in cloud, there stands the second monument. It is a tall and splendid eighteenth-century obelisk, and it commemorates a Scottish seigneur named Sir John Malcolm, who went from these parts long ago to become Governor of Bombay. It stands there just as one imagines he might have stood himself, calm, assured and high-flown, impervious to wind, mist, hail and time, the very figure of Scottishness.

Over the shoulder of MacDiarmid, as it were, stands Malcolm in the mist. The juxtaposition of the two, the one so rooted in reality, the other so unforgettable of image, seems a fitting metaphor to conclude

THE QUIRANG, ISLE OF SKYE

the text of this book: but for what lies beyond them both, in the air and the light and the numen of Scotland's visionary realm, look at the pictures – or look at the place.

But let me hear, in some far land, a kindred voice sing out, 'O why left I my hame?' and it seems at once as if no beauty under the kind heavens, and no society of the wise and good, can repay me for my absence from the country . . . I will say it fairly, it grows on me with every year: there are no stars so lovely as Edinburgh streetlamps.
ROBERT LOUIS STEVENSON

GLEN AFFRIC, HIGHLAND